# *The* EGYPTIAN JUKEBOX

## A Conundrum Created by
# NICK BANTOCK

A BYZANTIUM BOOK

VIKING

VIKING
Published by the Penguin Group
Penguin Books USA Inc., 375 Hudson Street,
New York, New York 10014, U.S.A.
Penguin Books Ltd, 27 Wrights Lane,
London W8 5TZ, England
Penguin Books Australia Ltd, Ringwood,
Victoria, Australia
Penguin Books Canada Ltd, 10 Alcorn Avenue,
Toronto, Ontario, Canada M4V 3B2
Penguin Books (N.Z.) Ltd, 182–190 Wairau Road,
Auckland 10, New Zealand
Penguin Books Ltd, Registered Offices:
Harmondsworth, Middlesex, England

First published in 1993 by Viking Penguin,
a division of Penguin Books USA Inc.

10 9 8 7 6 5 4 3 2

Copyright © Nick Bantock/Byzantium Books, 1993

*Library of Congress Cataloging in Publication Data*
Bantock, Nick.
    The Egyptian Jukebox: a conundrum/
    created by Nick Bantock.
            p.          cm.
    ISBN 0-670-84944-8
    I. Title.
    PR6052.A54E39   1993
    823'.914—dc20       92-35790

Printed and bound in Japan
Set in Garamond 3
Design: Barbara Hodgson/Byzantium Books
Editors: Cassia Farkas, Michael Jacobs
Production: Roni Axelrod
Photography: © Robert Keziere, 1993

Byzantium Books gratefully acknowledges the follow-
ing, who generously donated their precious treasures
to *The Egyptian Jukebox*:
Sarah Allen, Harry Bantock, Brad Cameron,
Gerry Eckford, Carol Fancy, David Gay, Alex Hass,
Robert Keziere, Eileen Schmidt, Peggy Thompson,
Saeko Usukawa

The Egyptian Jukebox is a wondrous-quirky museum cabinet. It was built by the eccentric millionaire Hamilton Hasp, who used his ineffable wealth to indulge his passions—carpentry, painting, acquiring odd artifacts, and, as he put it, "cunningly contriving conundrums."

The Jukebox embodies all of Hasp's skills and is the last and most enigmatic of his fabrications. It is a three-dimensional mystery housed in a splendid wooden cabinet of 10 drawers, which are filled with items carefully selected from his bizarre museum collection. Although these items seem randomly jumbled, they have been positioned with care, in order to lay down a trail of clues—clues that answer a question.

On the box's inscription plate Hasp invites the viewer to solve the riddle:
*Where do my worlds join?*

In addition to the visual and written clues there came a vocal assistance. Upon opening any of the drawers the Jukebox lit up, whilst a disc deep in the cabinet's belly began to play a recording of Hamilton Hasp telling a story—a singularly perplexing tale from his years of travel.

This book has been published with the kind permission of Tanis Hasp, Hamilton's only daughter and the present owner of the Jukebox. It is both a biographical testament to her father's ingenuity, and the first chance for those outside the family's circle to pit their wits against the old fox, who disappeared shortly after the Jukebox's completion. It is Tanis Hasp's belief that her father left a clue within the cabinet that may throw light on his whereabouts.

We have transcribed Hasp's stories, given you photographs of the inside of the drawers, and printed the inscription and cue notes that were found pasted to the underside of each drawer.

With the relevant information before you, you may be be able to succeed where others have failed, by solving the mystery of *The Egyptian Jukebox.*

Inscribed on the front of *The Egyptian Jukebox* are the following words:

*Where do my worlds join?*

HORUS
the falcon

SEKHMET
the lion

THOTH
the baboon

SET
the crocodile

AMON
the ram

ANUBIS
the jackal

PTAH
the magician

HATHOR
the cow

TAUERET
the hippo

BAST
the cat

The gods stand upright and give latitude.
From the yarns pluck golden songs to string across.
With this grid you may now navigate *The Egyptian Jukebox.*

Ten drawers—ten small solutions—and an answer.

My first memories were not of the United States, where I was born, but of Egypt, where my parents had taken up residence. They were archeologists, seekers amongst the tombs of the Valley of the Kings. To some they were scientists, to others no more than a new breed of grave robbers. To me they were the grown-ups I saw just before I went to bed.

As their only child, I spent much of the time amusing myself with the smaller archeological finds that I was able to get out of the library cabinet with the broken lock. Of course, my parents didn't leave me entirely to my own devices. For company I had my cats, and for my needs there was Ashraf, my servant. Ashraf's ancestors had lived and died in the Valley for thousands of years, which meant she had a strong feeling for the land and its contents. Consequently, she was somewhat disturbed by my choice of playthings. However, out of fondness for me, she never actually forbade me to touch the tomb treasures. Something my parents surely would have done had I not carefully replaced everything nightly before their return.

One evening I was sitting examining a small doll one of the diggers and dusters had unearthed the previous day, when there was a knock at the door.

Ashraf put down her polishing rag and padded across the carpeted floor, muttering about "interruptions." From the other side of the room I could hear a heavily muffled voice speaking to her urgently. I was curious and started towards the door, but Ashraf turned and intercepted me. As she bent towards me, I could see her face was chalk white. In her most serious tone she told me that I had to give back the doll. I looked beyond her shoulder to the heavily robed figure in the doorway.

Whoever it was stood in shadow, and I would have had no idea who wanted my toy had not a passing gendarme's lamp illuminated the depths of the visitor's hood. It was that fleeting view that persuaded me to hand over the doll without question. Once Ashraf had firmly closed and bolted the door behind the stranger, she started to shake uncontrollably. When she regained her composure, she earnestly instructed me never to speak of the events of the last few minutes. And should my parents ask about the doll, I was to say I knew nothing.

Usually I would have been shocked to have Ashraf ask me to lie. Not, however, on this occasion, for I had glimpsed the dusty gray bandages that swathed the face of the figure in our doorway.

23 24 25 26 27 28 29 30 31 32 33 34 35 36 37 38 39 40 41
receive
be Sold
near Petersfield
G 59
N 31

# DRAWER 1

*Clue page*

# Ln7 Wd11 / Ln26 Wd4

24 May '69

AT THE CROSSING BETWEEN U FROM THE PILLAR AND B FROM THE ROOF,

TRAVEL AT 5 O'CLOCK TO THE SCARAB.

REMOVE TO ITS NEAREST SIBLING.

HEAD DUE N. TO THE PASS AND DEDUCT FROM THE PASSWORD THE ROYAL AT 21.

## *You are now in possession of the fifth.*

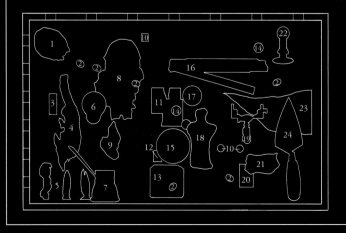

| | | | |
|---|---|---|---|
| 1 | Brass sleeper | 13 | Tobacco box |
| 2 | Scarab | 14 | Egyptian coinage |
| 3 | Cleopatra tab | 15 | Carnarvon's ink pot |
| 4 | Tomb door casing | 16 | Carter's rule |
| 5 | Unidentified remains | 17 | Disc chronometer |
| 6 | Clay lamp | 18 | Miniature mummy |
| 7 | Coffee maker | 19 | Swivel compass holder |
| 8 | Head of King Djoser | 20 | Key plate |
| 9 | Section of wood flower | 21 | Seal of King Sum-Mu |
| 10 | B #s | 22 | PWT stamp |
| 11 | Entrance tickets | 23 | Nubian parchment |
| 12 | 32M stamp | 24 | Maspero's trowel |

The scream was not piercing, it was the whispered cry of a soul familiar with its agony. I heard it only once, but it was one of those sounds I can never forget. I was young and had gone to Paris to experience the Bastille Day festivities. Not wishing to return to Boston immediately, I had lingered with a mind to explore and bask in the Gallic July sun.

On my fifth morning I headed for Notre-Dame, the great cathedral that so dominates the city, and within seconds of entry was lost to its cavernous glory. I had determined to copy Quasi-modo and comb every inch of the building, but the afternoon found me well short of my chosen task, and it was getting quite late in the day before I began ascending the last staircase open to the public. Tiredness was clawing at my calf muscles, and mid-flight I stopped to rest.

For five minutes I sat slumped in weariness, carelessly watching a narrow shaft of light meander across the uneven wall. Just as I was in the process of rising, I noticed the shaft had illuminated a letter "A" deeply scratched into the wall. I waited a little longer and was rewarded with a second letter—this time an "N." I waited still further, and one by one the remaining letters came—"ΑΓΚΗ." I speak no Greek, but I have read Victor Hugo and I knew that I had rediscovered his missing "FATALITY" inscription.

I reached up, wanting to touch the word and confirm that I had not been subject to some form of illusion. I am excessively tall, yet stretching on tiptoe my fingers barely reached the letters. I extended myself a little too far and my balance eluded me for a moment. To steady myself I threw out my left arm into the darkness of a permanent shadow. Having reestablished my footing, I became aware that my flail-ing hand had come to rest on a hidden ledge. I felt its length cautiously and came down with a small, and ancient, child's shoe.

The very moment I brought it into the sunlight, the stony silence was broken by that pathetic cry I mentioned previously. Do not ask me why, for I do not know, but I could not find it in me to replace the shoe or turn it over to the cathedral authori-ties, as I rightly should have. Irrationally, I believed that by removing La Esmeralda's shoe I could ease the hunchback's pained spirit.

ΑΝΑΓΚΗ

# DRAWER 2

## *Clue page*

## Ln2 Wd13 / Ln16 Wd5 / Ln29 Wd12

1 January '66

FROM THE BOOKSELLER'S COIN, TRAVEL THROUGH THE SUBWAY CIRCLE TO

THE SHIELD. HEAD UP THE VERTICAL UNTIL OBSTRUCTED.

GO W. PAST A SMALL WEAPON UNTIL YOU REACH THE DIAGONAL

BETWEEN R FROM THE GODS AND THE FIRST E FROM THE SONG.

### *You are now in possession of the eighth.*

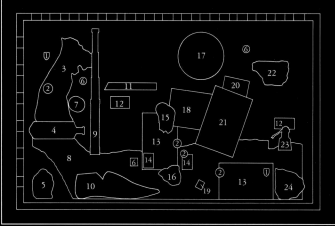

| | |
|---|---|
| 1 Town shield | 13 Notre-Dame card |
| 2 Franc | 14 Reims Cathedral stamp |
| 3 Gargoyle | 15 Tooth stone |
| 4 Three-sided bottle | 16 Pipe head |
| 5 The Hunchback | 17 Louis lion |
| 6 B #s | 18 Bookseller card |
| 7 Corridor candle | 19 Uncork |
| 8 City map | 20 The captains four |
| 9 Hugo's scope | 21 Street guide |
| 10 Shoe tree | 22 False alchemist's clay |
| 11 Fatality | 23 Black Pelican |
| 12 Train ticket | 24 Broken King |

I am of the conviction that one cannot perfect an art or a craft without first gaining sympathy for the tools of one's trade. It was with this creed in mind that I set out to spend a month in the Orient with the intention of learning a little about the mysteries of Chinese brush and Japanese paper making.

To get into China was difficult. I wasted five days in Hong Kong before bribery and my influential contacts gained me permission to stay for a week on the mainland with a master brush maker. The week was uneventful, although I did learn more in seven days than in my previous ten years. I speak none of the Chinese languages, but simply by watching I felt I was feasting on a banquet of craft wisdom.

For the remainder of my study period I went off to Kurotani, a mountain village northwest of Kyoto, to learn something of traditional paper making. The Kurotani paper makers were open and willing to show me anything I wished to know. So in my best poor Japanese I asked about everything. I tried my hand at picking and mixing and skimming and pressing, and found out that even the simplest-looking tasks required a great deal of skill.

One afternoon I came across a tiny strip of paper hanging on the elders' wall. I inquired, and was told that it was spider paper and that it could be made only on one night of the year. They also informed me that if I wished, I would be able to witness the paper's making, as the ceremony of the Night of Spiders was three days hence. I tried not to wish the days away, but I was impatient to see this intriguing-sounding ritual.

On the evening of the Night of Spiders, a pulp was prepared and ladled into a frame placed on a flat rock behind the village. At seven, with no cloud in the sky and darkness falling, all but the very young and very old climbed the mountain path to a ledge poised some twenty feet above the pulp frame. With warm saki and blankets we settled down to wait in a hushed huddle. I had been told what to expect, but when it came I was still caught off guard. The first few spiders came crawling from the east, and they approached the pulp with caution, circling the frame like scouts. Then a few minutes later they all came, hundreds of them, from the tiny to the giant. They poured onto the pulp and began to dance. No, not dance, rather ice skate—with spinning and sliding movements that grew faster and faster. As they skated they left silver trails in their wake. It seemed to go on forever, yet it must have been no longer than five minutes before they remounted the frame and disappeared over the rock edge from whence they came.

We stood, stretched, and silently made our way down to the pulp. It was a stunning sight—a silver network of the finest thread crisscrossed every inch of the pulp's surface. I asked the man next to me, "When will it be dried and pressed?"

He replied, "Not until tomorrow. It has yet to absorb moonshine."

"What was in the pulp mixture that attracted the spiders?" I asked, a mite too innocently. He smiled and, with a twinkle in his eye, replied, "Forgive me, but some things even the most honorable of barbarians must never know."

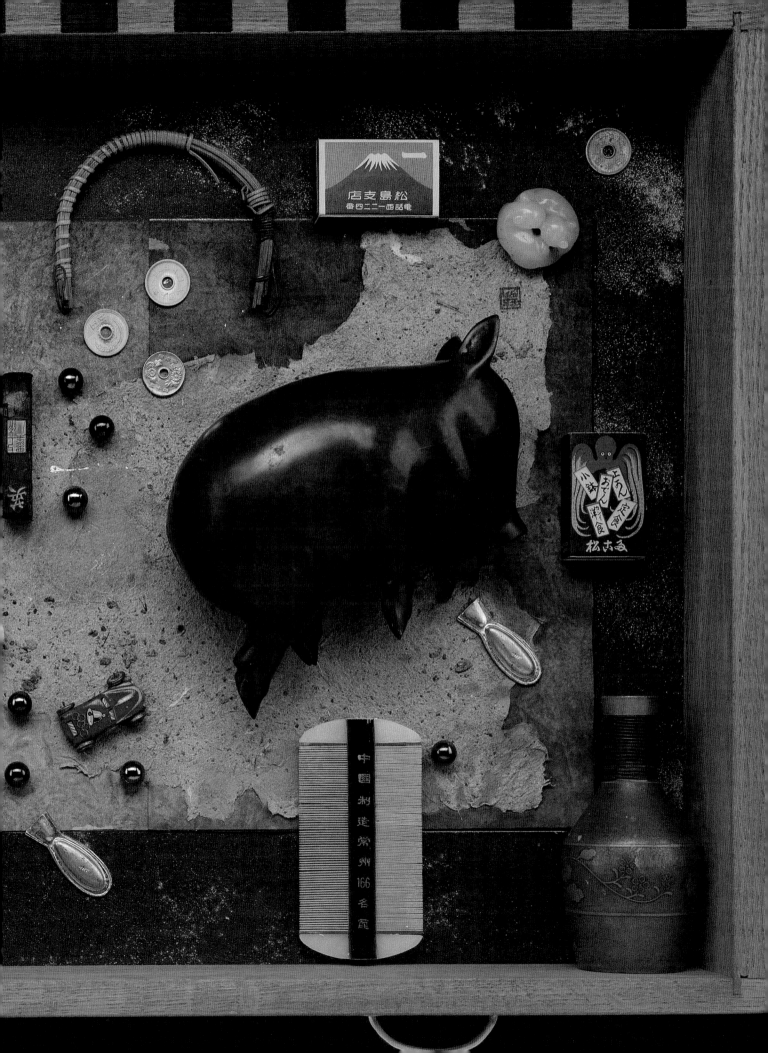

# DRAWER 3

*Clue page*

## Ln5 Wd2 / Ln11 Wd10 / Ln15 Wd8 / Ln25 Wd14

7 November '65

DROP DOWN FROM THE HOLE IN THE MIDDLE OF THE SONG'S WATERY VAPOR UNTIL YOU ARRIVE AT ONE OF THE 23 SPHERES. JUMP TO ITS FARTHEST COUNTERPART, LIFT UP TO THE COLDBLOODED VERTEBRATE, MOVE PORT SIDE TO THE PILLAR, DROP TWO LETTERS, AND THINK BACK TO THAT WHICH COMES IMMEDIATELY BEFORE.

*You are now in possession of the second.*

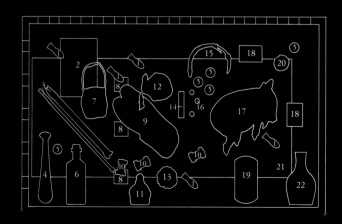

| | |
|---|---|
| 1 Silverfish | 12 Nest |
| 2 Lady Moonspider | 13 Buff dragon |
| 3 Master brushes | 14 Ink stick |
| 4 Pulp pestle | 15 Teapot handle |
| 5 Yen | 16 Oil marbles |
| 6 Fake rainbow web | 17 Iron pig |
| 7 Powder basket | 18 Matchboxes |
| 8 Revenue stamps | 19 Fine sift comb |
| 9 Toed slipper | 20 Kissing cousins |
| 10 Toy transport | 21 New Year paper |
| 11 Black Buddha | 22 Tot Nes pot |

For me, gaining my first pilot's license meant a hitherto unrealized freedom of movement. I could hop from Belgium to Spain, or Boston to Newfoundland without restriction. After a few years of flying short trips, I considered myself ready to take on something more daring. I decided on a solo exploration of the South Seas. Starting in northern Australia, I would fly Lucrecia, my Gypsy Moth seaplane, in a loop, visiting as many of the islands as I could before ending up in New Guinea.

Map distances are one thing; flying them on your own is quite another. My nice, neat loop plan was soon discarded, as my daily choice of direction became more random. I found myself lost on so many occasions it started to become a habit. It got to the point where I'd fly for as long as I felt like, then head for the nearest radio contact. More than once I almost ran out of fuel. Eventually I had an extra tank built on, which slowed me down but pretty much guaranteed safe arrival . . . somewhere.

It was through this non-specific navigation method that I found myself, late one afternoon, on a small island east of the Marshalls. I landed in a shallow cove and swam to the beach. I'd learned that this was a refreshing way of cleansing my mind and body of the cockpit's stuffiness. When I stepped on shore and got a closer look at the vegetation, I found the place to be most peculiar. I recognized only half the plants, and many of the insects were new to me. Even the birds' songs sounded unfamiliar.

I had heard it said that not all the South Seas islands had been mapped, and that there was always a chance of finding unrecorded flora and fauna. The reality of finding myself on such an island was unnerving. Naturally I was curious, but I also felt burdened by an obligation to be a serious observer. I decided my exploration would have to be cursory, as I had to be back on the Marshalls by nightfall. I found a freshwater stream and followed it inland for around a mile. It took me to a clearing and the crumbled remains of an old stone house. Amidst the ruins stood a circle of charred ground with a stack of carved driftwood sculptures at its center. They had been piled there without care, some being broken, and were undoubtedly ready for burning. I looked around, saw no one, and impulsively picked up the most striking sculpture. Then in an act of fair trade, guilt, or maybe superstition, I pulled off my wristwatch and placed it on top of the remaining pile. I made my way back to the beach, gathered a bagful of shells, and then swam back to Lucrecia.

On my return flight I had every intention of reverse-plotting the island's position, but I hit a storm and was thrown about all over the place, and by the time I made land I had lost my bearings. When I came to study the powerful carving in detail, I realized how hard it was to see where nature had left off and man had taken over. I wanted more of the stack. I wanted to know who made them and why they were being burned. For weeks I tried desperately to relocate the island and could not. I had lost it. In retrospect, I'm glad I couldn't find it again, for now it remains to me the most personal of mysteries.

# DRAWER 4

*Clue page*

# Ln33 Wd12

27 January '73

ADD THE EYE PROTECTORS' # TO THE RITUAL ROTATOR'S # AND DEDUCT FROM THE FEMALE BORGIA'S #. THE RESULTANT # GIVES YOU YOUR STARTING POSITION. ·GRID LEFT FOR A LETTER, GRID UP FOR ANOTHER (TRIPLICATE IT), ADD ALL 4 TO THE SUN GOD AND REMOVE FROM THE OBJECT BETWEEN 11 AND 19.

## *You are now in possession of the tenth.*

| | |
|---|---|
| 1 Island shells | 12 B #s |
| 2 G moth grid | 13 Barbs |
| 3 Small marker crab | 14 Papua stamp |
| 4 Flying goggles | 15 Worm stick sculpture |
| 5 Etched gourd | 16 Peg starfish |
| 6 Seaplane smoke card | 17 Sea tree |
| 7 Ceremonial spinning top | 18 Tattooed warrior card |
| 8 Tortoise shell | 19 Dragon skull sculpture |
| 9 Torso root | 20 Moth |
| 10 Veridia feather | 21 Lucrecia |
| 11 Gypsy headphones | 22 Ocean map |

The London Underground is a relatively safe and mild place to while away one's time, or so I thought. I'd been traveling around the inner city's Circle Line since mid-morning, watching the platform people, and making jottings in my sketch-book. During the day my fellow passengers were mostly de-mobbed servicemen job-hunting and housewives on day trips. By evening the young entertainment seekers were abroad, pink and giggly with excitement. But as eleven o'clock came and went, the suburb dwellers removed to Ongar, Acton, and Cockfosters, and the light in the carriage grew whiter, giving my few remaining companions the pallor of sour milk.

I had positioned myself in the last seat in the row, the one next to the center double doors. When the doors slid back over the window, the two parallel panes of glass reflected back a double image—four eyes, nose superimposed over mouth, and mouth in neck. Strangers to the "tube" have been known to catch sudden sight of this visual trick and become frightened. Not I . . . I thought it comical.

At five to midnight I was the carriage's sole remaining rider, and as Liverpool Street was the next stop, I readied myself for dismounting. The train had paused in the tunnel immediately before the station, as it had done consistently throughout its circuits, and I stared once again at my double image. It seemed darker, more intense than before. I blinked, but it was undoubtedly more defined, and although still my portrait it had become repulsive, with eyes of fire. The wait became interminable as the face, now wolflike, seemed to salivate and leer. The face moved forward, its nose pressed against the glass, and its yellow teeth scraped the outside of the window.

I glanced left and right to make absolutely certain there was no one else in the carriage who might help me. I was alone. The seat opposite, the one below the face, started to bulge and quiver. My distorted reflection was trying to enter the carriage. The seat began shaking violently, and I could tell it was only a matter of seconds before the odious creature would break into the carriage and be at my throat. Then the train gave a jolt, we spurted forward, and the face was lost in the station lights.

We came to a halt, the doors slid open, and for half a second I gaped at the passive seat opposite me. Then I fled. It may be considered cowardly, but never again on my subsequent visits to England's capital would anyone be able to induce me down those long escalators to the dark tunnels of the London Underground.

# DRAWER 5

*Clue page*

## Ln8 Wd6 / Ln21 Wd6 / Ln24 Wd4

31 July '67

MIDWAY BETWEEN THE FIRST PEELER AND THE CHAR RECEPTACLE IS A LEATHER

CHERRY. TRAVEL N.E. FROM ITS CENTER TOWARDS THE TRIDENT HOLDER AT GRID BH,

STOP ON THE 2ND #. BETWEEN THAT #'S ROMAN EQUIVALENT AND THE

LETTER BENEATH THE TRAVELER'S INVERTED # COMES THAT WHICH YOU NEED.

### *You are now in possession of the fourth.*

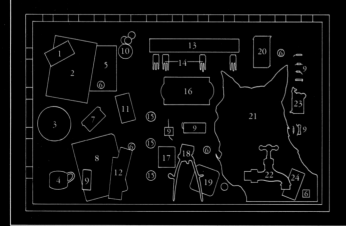

| | |
|---|---|
| 1 Police signal card | 13 Warden's door sign |
| 2 Circle Line sketchbook | 14 Warden's teeth plugs |
| 3 Cricket ball | 15 Donkey jacket buttons |
| 4 R. Lee's mug | 16 Lift switch |
| 5 Lotto sheet | 17 Book of matches |
| 6 B #s | 18 Barber's clippers |
| 7 Snuff box & mouth organ | 19 Meccano tin |
| 8 Walking guide | 20 Guard's box |
| 9 Underground mufflers | 21 Liverpool Street wolf |
| 10 GB coins | 22 Tube tap |
| 11 Fireman card | 23 Brass lighter |
| 12 Festival tickets | 24 The traveler |

Chess, so I've read, was first played in India. I have a fondness for both the game and the country. India has a way of demonstrating that time has different speeds, and chess, unless played against the clock, offers a similar experience. One can disappear into a reverie of computation that is almost endless and quite beautiful. Marcel Duchamp once told me that he considered chess the nearest thing to aesthetic and spiritual perfection. He insisted that the pieces themselves were capable of containing a pure life force, and that they should be handled with reverence. I considered his statement an elegant abstraction, until one summer in 1949.

I was staying in the house of a friend in the hills above Simla. The house was large and colonially comfortable, with fine furnishings that included an exquisite hardwood inlaid chess board. On the board were ivory pieces as fine to touch as to look at. My friend had been away for a few days and was not due back until the following week. I had taken to playing myself at chess to occupy the time until her return. One evening I became tired mid-game and decided to stop, reasoning that I could just as easily finish the game in the morning. I made my last move—a white, king-side castle—and then went to my bed.

After breakfast the following day, I returned to the board to find that a black piece had been moved in a far from arbitrary way. The Queen's knight had been developed to a dangerous position. My reaction was to assume one of the house staff was a secret player. However, when questioned, they all denied any knowledge of the game. When, the next morning, black had again replied to my last move, I decided to look into the matter further. That night, after pretending to retire, I returned to a partially curtained alcove no more than three feet from the board. I settled myself in a comfortable chair, cradled a large glass of brandy, and waited for what I expected to be the entrance of a cunning servant.

By two o'clock no one had come, and I was having trouble staying awake. I fixed my gaze on the board and considered the game, which was at a critical point. I noticed that a black pawn was not fully on its square. My heavy eyes closed for a few moments, and when I reopened them the pawn appeared even farther out of its place. I looked harder, and became aware of two things. First, that if the black pawn were to be moved into the square it was touching, it would unhinge white's defense (something I had totally missed earlier on), and second, the pawn was very gradually moving into that square of its own volition.

I sat spellbound until black had completed its move. I then stretched out from behind the curtain to advance the white queen's pawn. Over the next half hour I played the game out with the self-moving pieces and was soundly beaten, as I was in all subsequent games. When my friend returned a few days later, I told her of the phantom board and how it had continually defeated me. "That does not surprise me" was her casual reply. "I never win against it either."

# DRAWER 6

*Clue page*

## Ln21 Wd4 / Ln28 Wd2 / Ln38 Wd7

16 September '72

BLACK TO MOVE. PAWN TAKES PAWN. FROM ITS NEW HOME # DEDUCT THE # OF THE

DEAD MONARCH. USING THE RESULT COUNT CAST FIGURES FROM THE RIGHT.

TRAVEL N. TO THE SONG'S LETTER. FIND ITS TWIN ON THE PILLAR. DROP DOWN A

LETTER AND HEAD E. INTO THE DRAWER UNTIL YOU COME TO THE INITIAL LETTER.

## *You are now in possession of the first.*

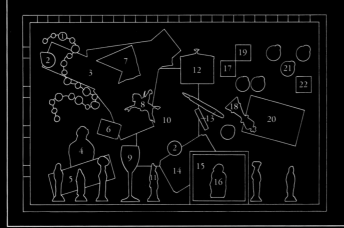

| | |
|---|---|
| 1 Dung beads | 12 India tea caddy |
| 2 Cone men | 13 Scribe's pen |
| 3 Five correspondences | 14 Angel letter |
| 4 The player | 15 Astronomy pigeon hole |
| 5 The sixth letter | 16 Stone thumb sucker |
| 6 Incense box | 17 KR3 |
| 7 Sealed move | 18 Fallen King |
| 8 Horse soldier | 19 KKt2 |
| 9 Bishop's goblet | 20 Young India card |
| 10 Bone crunchers | 21 Queen's pawn on QP3 |
| 11 Six caste figures | 22 QB4 |

Having little or no success acquiring high-quality pre-Columbian art in Mexico City, I decided to move south, to Colombia. Before I left I bought a number of modern items that, in my view, were far superior to the dubious and low-grade relics the dealers had been offering me. A small sculpture of a devil-headed snake, encircling an apple, especially took my fancy. I am not normally fond of Christian symbolism, but this serpent had a particularly disrespectful quality that pleased me greatly.

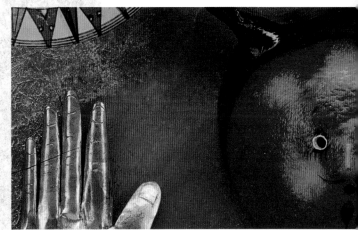

On my fourth day in Colombia, I was traveling through a seemingly unpopulated district when my Jeep died. I tried everything I could think of, but the engine remained utterly inert. I radioed for help and was told someone would be out in the morning and that I should just make camp and sit tight. I pitched tent about fifty yards from the road, on a soft, grassy knoll shielded by a half moon of trees, and went hunting for firewood.

I wasn't sure what wild animals stalked those parts, so as night began to fall I lit my (probably unnecessarily large) bonfire. The flame from my match transferred easily to the woodpile, and in seconds I had a heart-warming blaze. I sat on a log and watched the flames whilst my skillet of supper heated. The firewood I'd gathered came from the fallen branches of large silver-barked trees whose origins were unknown to me; however my choice had obviously been good, as not only did the wood throw out plenty of heat, but also gave off a very pleasant scent. Too pleasant, as I was soon to find out.

After a period of dreamy contemplation, I realized I was getting very light-headed, which I put down to a cross between altitude and Boy Scout exhilaration. Then, by the time I realized I'd undergone a physical reaction, I was too deeply euphoric to move myself. I have no idea how long I smiled stupidly into the flames before they began to take shape. It could have been minutes, or it could have been the better part of the night. The movement began with a swirling at the fire's purring, yellow core; then, as the scarlet outer edges were sucked in, the conical mass transformed itself into a coiled snake.

In my semi-detached state, I gazed without surprise or fear at the spectacle before me. Even when it grew threefold in size and reached up into the tree, to pluck a giant apple, I still grinned benignly. Its head, which had now taken the shape of a cadmium red devil, floated above me, proffering the apple. I'm sure I would have reached out and clasped it thankfully with both hands had not an arrow from the darkness nicked my earlobe on its way to skewering the apple and piercing the snake through the throat. With the blow, the serpent shriveled and dissolved back into the fire, and I found myself sighing in disappointment as I slid quietly from my perch to the warm earth.

With daybreak I awoke, not fuzzy brained, but clear and full of well-being. This state was only slightly threatened by the annoying little cut at the base of my ear and by the way the mechanic looked at me as if I were a lousy practical joker when the Jeep started on the first twist of the key.

# DRAWER 7

*Clue page*

## Ln19 Wd8 / Ln42 Wd17

12 January '74

FOLLOW DEATH'S POINTED TIP UP SHAFT TO HORN'S CROSS. HEAD N.E. TO THE EYE,

THEN W. TILL YOU REACH A SPOT BELOW H FROM THE SONG. GO DIAGONALLY

ACROSS 10 THROUGH MEPHISTO UNTIL YOU REACH THE BORDERED HEAD.

AIM N. YOUR ANSWER SITS ATOP $3^2$ X 2.

### *You are now in possession of the ninth.*

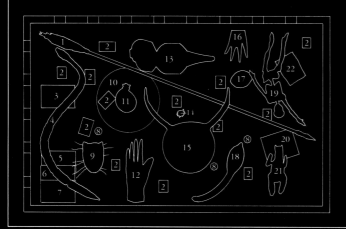

| 1 Straight snake arrow | 12 Silver hand |
|---|---|
| 2 Postage | 13 Compass |
| 3 Three of clubs | 14 Semi-Sol |
| 4 Wooden rattler | 15 Mephisto |
| 5 Three of cups | 16 Second hand |
| 6 Knave of swords | 17 Peacock's eye |
| 7 Five of swords | 18 Runt snake |
| 8 B #s | 19 Death's bones |
| 9 Mad cat head | 20 Ten pesos |
| 10 Snake-centered NESW | 21 Tigerman suit |
| 11 Devil snake and apple | 22 Plastic holy bag |

Sitting in a café in Florence one afternoon, I became engaged in a conversation with a laconic old painter introduced to me as Mack. In a rather elliptical fashion we came around to discussing the quattrocento, and I asked him if he knew of any strange tales from that period, adding that I was fond of mysteries. He considered awhile and then replied (in a rich Edinburgh brogue that I will not attempt to emulate) that he knew of one that might pique my interest. This is the story he related.

"Verrocchio—whom history unkindly records principally as Leonardo's master—was a great sculptor, as you, being a student of the Renaissance, would know. His dedication and seriousness stemmed from an unfortunate incident during his teens. Coming home one dusk, he got into a stone-throwing mock battle with some apprentice masons. It was not meant maliciously, but one of his egglike rocks struck an adversary on the forehead, killing him outright. Verrocchio, though arrested, was released on the grounds of unintentional homicide, but the incident scarred him deeply.

"Many years later, on being commissioned to produce a marble figure of *Young David Victorious Over Goliath*, he became overwhelmed with the task. Not because it was beyond his capacity as an artist, but because he could not bring himself to sculpt a youth with a sling and stone. He worked on other, less important commissions. He struggled with the studio's accounts. In fact, he did anything he could to avoid *Young David*. Then, when it seemed he would have to renege on his commitment or hand it over to one of his assistants, a second incident occurred.

"He was returning home late from a dinner with friends when he found himself about to pass the place where he had inadvertently killed the young mason. His usual practice of avoiding the street would have been time-consuming, and as he was very tired he put his head down and marched forward. On the exact spot where he had flung his missile many years before lay a broken knife. As he bent to pick it up, a stone the size of a fist came flying out of the darkness, smashing into the wall at the point where his head had been a half second earlier.

"Although Verrocchio was stunned and frightened, it gradually dawned on him that he had been released from his block, and also had hit upon a practical way to circumnavigate his artistic problem. When he returned to the studio he began work immediately on the figure of David, but, instead of a slingshot, the boy held a knife, and underneath his foot was the severed head of the enemy he had defeated in fair combat."

# DRAWER 8

*Clue page*

## Ln2 Wd9 / Ln19 Wd3 / Ln36 Wd16

11 October '59

IF THE CIRCLE AT THE TIP OF M'S OPENER ROLLS TO 4", THEN ASCENDS TO THE SONG,
IT MEETS THE SAME LETTER THAT APPEARS ON 2 B#S—DISCARD. OF THE B#S LEFT
CHOOSE THE CLOSEST TO HAND. ADD THE DIGITS TOGETHER TO GAIN THE
LIST #—TAKE AWAY THE # AND THE DIRECTION FINDER. YOU NEED WHAT REMAINS.

## *You are now in possession of the third.*

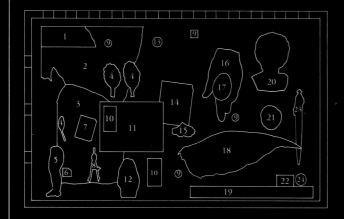

| | |
|---|---|
| 1 Saint Leo marble | 13 Sforza's eye |
| 2 Blue-line bone anatomy | 14 Crumbling man |
| 3 Verrocchio's *Young David* | 15 Golden fig |
| 4 Maquette trees | 16 David's plaster hand |
| 5 Discarded leg | 17 Egg stone |
| 6 State stamp | 18 Lone wing |
| 7 Profile matchbox | 19 Black and red ruler |
| 8 Space compass | 20 Young Goliath |
| 9 B #s | 21 Disc and Ferrel |
| 10 Bandaged head cards | 22 Express post |
| 11 Dissolving still | 23 M's letter opener |
| 12 Greek head | 24 Silver lire |

Before I say more about my encounter, I want to make it clear that my visit to the bordello was an accident. I had been strolling the streets around Jackson Square for an hour or so, searching for jazz memorabilia, when I noticed her. She was, in retrospect, strangely attired. But New Orleans, more than any other city in the United States, forgives the exotic and, to be frank, it was not her clothing that caught my attention.

She had, without doubt, the most unutterably beautiful face I had ever seen. On another occasion, hurried by duty, I might have gawked and turned away, unable to bear her exquisiteness. But on that dreamy spring evening I was a romantic with time on my hands, and I simply followed her like a docile lamb behind its shepherdess. She must have been aware of my presence, yet she neither slowed nor hastened as she glided serenely along. After two or three blocks she turned into a house with a dark blue door, and I followed without consideration.

I found myself in an overly furnished room full of men smoking and women in their undergarments. It took me a few seconds to realize the nature of the establishment, and by the time it had sunk in, it was too late to turn and walk out. And anyway, I had relocated my shepherdess now, sitting demurely on the other side of the room, slightly apart from the raucous goings-on. I am shy, and could not bring myself to go over to her, so I sat at the nearest table and watched whilst I sipped the bourbon that had been placed in front of me. I stayed there for an hour, unable to understand why no men approached her. Far less attractive women had been escorted up the stairs on a number of occasions. It was almost as if I was the only one who could see her. I was in a quandary. I wanted to meet her, talk with her, but I didn't want to buy her services—that would have been crude and somehow irreverent.

In the end I arose, smiled sheepishly, and left. I didn't want to lose sight of her but I could think of nothing else to do. Back in my room I undressed, switched off the light, and climbed into bed, lonely and rather sorry for myself in the shuttered darkness. A minute or so later, and without warning, I felt someone's soft lips on my cheek. I reached up, but no one was there. As I was rising from my pillow, a quiet, throaty female voice whispered, "Lie still."

What does one do when someone who isn't there kisses you and tells you not to move? I had no idea, so I did as I was told. From her first touch I knew it was my bordello shepherdess, and her words confirmed it. She told me that she had come to me because I had not tried to buy her. That she had waited many years to meet one who would respect her. And that as a gesture of thanks she would perform the rights of the flesh without price. When I awoke, late the next morning, her smell was still in my nostrils, her velvet touch was still on my skin, but she was gone.

I returned to the house with the blue door and spoke with the Madame. I described my beautiful friend and asked to see her. The Madame became pale and deadly serious, telling me to pursue the matter no further, as I had recalled in perfect detail the Angel Vampire, devourer of more than thirty souls in less than a century. Involuntarily, my hand rose to feel my unmarked neck, and I remembered my angel's words: ". . . without price."

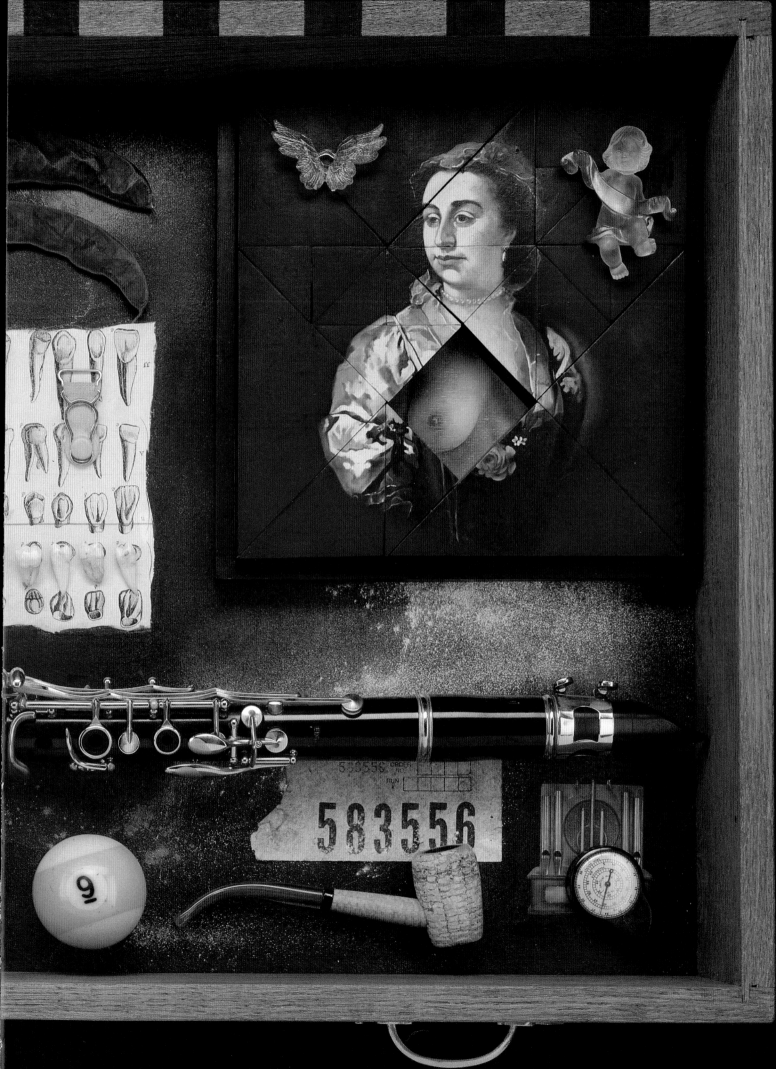

# DRAWER 9

*Clue page*

## Ln13 Wd5 / Ln37 Wd5

21 September '63

THE SUM OF THE TIME AND THE BALL, DEDUCTED FROM THE SUM OF THE CASE FILE
DIGITS PLUS THE STOCKING CLIP # MINUS THE BOOT EAR STUDS # GIVES THE # OF
UNWANTED LETTERS IN THE GOD'S NAME. DISPOSE OF THE HEADGEAR
WORN THE WRONG WAY AROUND. YOU REQUIRE WHAT IS LEFT OVER.

### *You are now in possession of the seventh.*

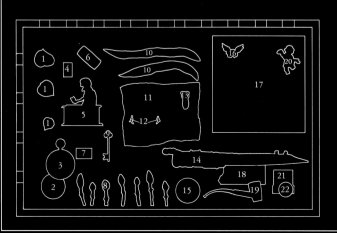

| | |
|---|---|
| 1 Chinese Lanterns | 12 Boot ear studs |
| 2 Wurlitzer circle | 13 Stocking clip |
| 3 Chronometer | 14 Clarinet section |
| 4 The Raven | 15 #9 pool ball |
| 5 Ebony ghoul toy | 16 Angel's wings |
| 6 Tin taxi | 17 The Angel Vampire |
| 7 U.S. airmail stamp | 18 Case file number |
| 8 Magnolia seed pods | 19 Corn pipe |
| 9 Jackson Street key | 20 Angel's body |
| 10 Honey Locust pods | 21 Wurlitzer organ |
| 11 Vampire teeth chart | 22 Meter |

When we were children, my young, credulous cousin and I were often told this story by our grandfather. When it became clear that the Tzar's enemies were going to win, he instructed his boot boy to take a small casket that had been with the Romanov family for six generations and smuggle it out of the country. The boy embarked on a long and tortuous journey in the hope of eluding any possible pursuers. The last stage of his escape route took him across the Caspian Sea, and, ironically, when he was finally safely out of Russia, he was cornered by pirates in a Persian bay. Before he could be captured, he hid the sealed box somewhere in the bay. The pirates took him far away, and he died of typhoid before he could return to retrieve the Tzar's treasure.

My cousin Matthew was certain that this was a true story and vowed to search for the casket when he was old enough. Years passed, and I assumed he'd forgotten all about it. Then one day he came to me saying that he'd researched the subject thoroughly and had pinned the possible hiding spot to one of four locations, and would I care to accompany him to the Caspian Sea? He knew only too well that it is not in my heart to turn down a mystery.

The boot boy had left a notebook (which my cousin had acquired after a protracted legal battle with a Greek shipping magnate), in which he hinted at the casket's whereabouts with cryptic sketches. The first two bays cartographically fit the drawings, but when we reached them, they were clearly wrong. The third was promising, but after a few days of study failed to live up to its initial promise. The last bay seemed to fit all the requirements, and we set about the task of unearthing our quarry. Our team, which consisted of five men and three women, photographed, measured, dug, and compared notes all the hours that daylight offered. We knew the Iranian authorities would never give us permission to hunt, and therefore we were there illegally. Although the area was remote, we wished to be gone as soon as possible.

Matthew felt certain the casket contained the Romanovs' five-pointed Abyssinian glass star, the center of which held a large, perfect pearl. I, however, being cynical of servant loyalty, favored a tin of boot polish and a thank-you note. It took us three weeks before we found the casket, in thick undergrowth and six feet down. We dug frantically through hard-pan clay and rock for ten hours, and then we slowed to a snail's pace. It was a time to be savored. No one whispered a word as Matthew sprang the lock and lifted the lid with enormous care. I can still see the look on his face as he lifted forth two rusty old tools—a hammer and a sickle.

# DRAWER 10

*Clue page*

## Ln18 Wd9 / Ln25 Wd8 / Ln31 Wd1

28 April '79

FIND THE SINGING SOLDIER. BETWEEN HIS HEAD AND THAT OF THE AQUATIC EQUUS
COMES ANOTHER'S HEAD. YOU ARE AT ONE END OF A STEEL BOW. FOLLOW IT
UNTIL YOU ARE CLOSE TO A CYCLOPTIC SNAKE. FROM THERE TRAVEL
THROUGH THE SOVIET OBSERVER TO THE SONG. DEDUCT FROM THE MORNING.

*You are now in possession of the sixth.*

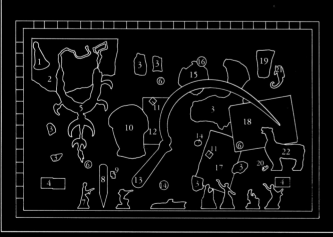

| | |
|---|---|
| 1 Alexander Bell | 12 Illuminated page |
| 2 CCCP corner page | 13 Scarlet sickle |
| 3 Rocks, various | 14 Persepolis blue glass |
| 4 Imperforate stamps | 15 Romanov clasps |
| 5 Bear claw necklace | 16 Lenin's eye (replica) |
| 6 B #s | 17 Expressionist cover |
| 7 Metal revolutionaries | 18 Red star letter mail |
| 8 Bullet plumb line | 19 Borderland fossil |
| 9 Communist Party badge | 20 Romanov pin |
| 10 Persian wood block | 21 Caspian seahorse |
| 11 Die | 22 Broken tail creature |

*For the solution to the mystery of*
The Egyptian Jukebox,
*please turn the page.*